OVERCOMING ANXIETY

How to deal with stress and panic

Written by Barbara Radomme
Translated by Rebecca Neal

Health and Wellbeing 50MINUTES.com

OVERCOMING ANXIETY

- **Problem:** for some people, the world around them is a constant source of fear and anxiety, while others only have these feelings in specific situations. Anxiety sufferers experience debilitating and frightening symptoms such as cold sweats, listlessness and heart palpitations. It is important to understand why these symptoms appear and take steps to break free of fear.
- **Aim:** to understand and overcome anxiety.
- **FAQs:**
  - I am constantly worried and stressed. Everything makes me anxious and this sometimes paralyses me. Is this normal?
  - If I am naturally anxious, is there really anything I can do about it, since it is a part of my temperament?
  - When I have a sudden anxiety attack, what can I do to calm down?
  - My partner is a very anxious person. What can I do to help them?

Our throat tightens, we struggle to breathe, our heart races, our skin is beaded with sweat and, all of a sudden, a gnawing, paralysing feeling of anxiety appears in the pit of our stomach and spreads throughout our body. We are immediately overwhelmed and feel that we are no longer in charge of our own body.

All of us are familiar with anxiety and have experienced it at one time or another: it emerges when we have to give a presentation, meet somebody new or deal with an unexpected phone call, or even during harmless everyday events such as nightfall or the silent emptiness of a Sunday afternoon. As long as these episodes are sporadic and bearable, there is nothing to worry about. However, when this feeling of anxiety becomes constant and intense and starts interfering with your everyday life, it is time to act! Do not let anxiety stop you from thriving. There are a range of simple solutions and tools you can use to halt its far-reaching effects. Whether you are working alone or with the support of others, and at home or within a group, there are plenty of tricks at your disposal.

In 50 minutes, you will discover where this gnawing discomfort comes from, learn about the warning signs and find advice and tips to finally stop anxiety from dictating your life. Do not give up: every problem has a solution.

WHAT IS ANXIETY?

STRESS, FEAR OR ANXIETY?

Although these terms may seem quite similar at first glance and are often used interchangeably, they actually have different characteristics and effects. While stress and fear are normally temporary, anxiety is more insidious and casts a more or less constant shadow over sufferers.

Stress

Stress is a common and completely natural phenomenon which emerges in response to an event. It is a physiological reaction by our bodies which allows us to confront a challenging or threatening situation. However, in our modern societies, where we are constantly on the go and overwork is common, we are experiencing stress more and more, and it risks reaching unhealthy levels. Indeed, while occasional stress in particular situations is a positive, sometimes life-saving reaction, regular and persistent stress has destructive effects on our physical and mental health.

Fear

Fear is characterised by its intensity and by a certain relationship to reality. It results from the intense feeling that we are dealing with a threat that is vague and undefined, but rooted in reality. It is therefore temporary and context-dependent. Finally, while fear is undeniably a psychological sensation, it is expressed above all in physical symptoms: tremors, increased heart rate, and so on.

Anxiety

The Collins English Dictionary defines anxiety as "a state of uneasiness or tension caused by apprehension of possible future misfortune, danger, etc" or "a state of intense apprehension or worry often accompanied by physical symptoms such as shaking, intense feelings in the gut, etc". In other words, anxiety is an emotional state of nervous agitation, which can manifest itself in different forms and with varying degrees of intensity. Unlike fear, which appears suddenly and results in temporary mental and physical incapacity, anxiety does not stop us from getting on with our day-to-day lives, since it is a vaguer, but also more constant, state of worry. Although it is an unpleasant feeling, anxiety does not pose any health concerns as long as it remains mild. However, if we do not do anything to control the situation and overcome these negative emotions of constant pessimism and worry, it can develop into its pathological form, generalised anxiety disorder.

	Every day	Often	Rarely	Never
In the last two weeks, have you had difficulty falling or staying asleep?				
Do you struggle to concentrate?				
Do you feel tense, nervous or worried?				
Do you worry about the past or the future?				
If your friends are late meeting you, do you think that something has happened to them and try to call or text them every five minutes?				
Do you have nervous sensations like a lump in your throat, difficulty breathing, a racing heartbeat or a knot in your stomach?				
Do you struggle to not be constantly moving, do nothing and relax?				
Do your reactions to events tend to be exaggerated or impulsive?				

You mostly answered "every day": you are very often stressed and anxious, and it seems that these feelings take precedence over your life balance. Make sure that you do not let them overwhelm you too often. Feel free to follow the advice in this book and to ask a healthcare professional for help.

> **You mostly answered "often":** you have a tendency towards anxiety, but it is not debilitating for you on an everyday basis. However, do not hesitate explore the issue further, because nothing is stopping you from improving your quality of life.
>
> **You mostly answered "rarely":** you are rarely affected by anxiety. Of course, it still happens sometimes, but mainly in very stressful situations. You seem to be very good at managing your emotions, which enables you to stay in control in all situations.
>
> **You mostly answered "never":** you are incredibly composed, and anxiety is an unfamiliar feeling for you. Whether you are stressed or not, and whether you are dealing with a crisis or relaxing on holiday, your mood stays the same. This is better for your nerves, but do not forget that a little dose of adrenaline from time to time is beneficial, and sometimes even desirable.

ANXIETY DISORDERS

Anxiety disorders are a range of psychological illnesses characterised by a profound, intense and constant feeling of anxiety which is debilitating for the sufferer on an everyday basis. While classification may vary slightly between countries, the DSM-IV (*Diagnostic and Statistical Manual of Mental Disorders*) distinguishes between six particular forms: generalised anxiety disorder, panic disorder with or without agoraphobia, specific phobias, obsessive-compulsive disorder and post-traumatic stress disorder.

The thing that all these disorders have in common is that they affect the prefrontal cortex. This is the most evolved region of the brain and deals with its most abstract thoughts, such as predictions for the future, decision-making, problem-solving and the implementation of strategies. This region is also directly connected to the limbic lobe, which is responsible for emotions. This means that anxiety disorders affect both abstract thoughts and emotions. Anxiety therefore puts our overall health at risk.

The four regions of the brain

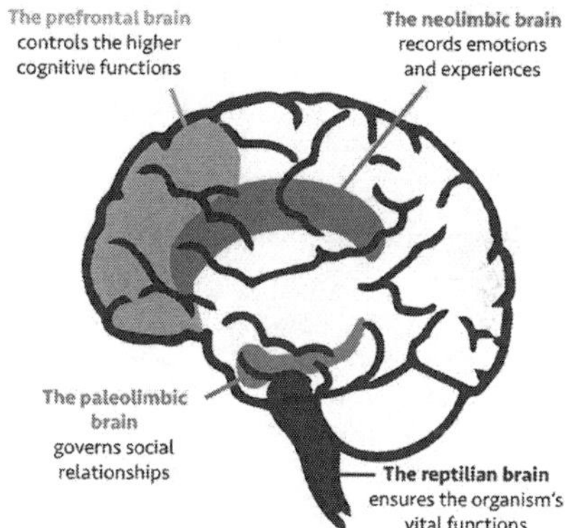

Generalised anxiety disorder (GAD)

Specialists make a clear distinction between mild, temporary anxiety and intense, chronic anxiety. For pathological
anxiety to be diagnosed, the patient must have been suffering from at least three of the following symptoms for a
minimum of six months:

- difficulty sleeping,
- tiredness,
- irritability,
- difficulty concentrating,
- agitation,

- muscle pains.

GAD is characterised by general, difficult-to-control anxiety and constant, exaggerated worrying about everyday events for no apparent reason. It is estimated that between 5 and 8% of the population in Western countries suffers from GAD, and woman are affected twice as much as men (Besançon, 1993: 41).

Panic disorder with or without agoraphobia

Panic disorder is characterised by recurring and unpredictable panic attacks during situations which present no real danger, and by the constant fear that these panic attacks will happen again. During a panic attack, the person experiences an intense, temporary feeling of anxiety, and presents physical symptoms that are typical of extreme situations (heart palpitations, trembling, feeling of suffocation, fainting, fear of going mad, and so on). If this disorder is accompanied by agoraphobia, the individual will be anxious about going to places that it might be difficult to escape from, and therefore where it will be difficult to get help if they start having a panic attack.

According to the DSM-IV, several characteristics need to appear together for the problem to be diagnosed as panic disorder:

- the individual must have experienced unexpected and recurring panic attacks (several over the course of the same month);
- these panic attacks must be accompanied by a constant

fear of experiencing further attacks;
* they must also be combined with worry about possible repercussions and consequences;
* they must result in major behavioural changes with the aim of preventing possible further attacks.

It should be noted that panic attacks are not caused by excessive alcohol or drug use and do not result from other mental problems or physical issues.

Social anxiety disorder

This illness, which is also known as social phobia, is described as excessive anxiety which emerges in the context of social relationships or in situations during which the individual may display symptoms of anxiety. This type of panic attack is lasting and continues until the individual has escaped the situation causing their anxiety. This leads them to adopt avoidant behaviour and break off all social contact.

The *Diagnostic and Statistical Manual of Mental Disorders* clearly outlines the specific features of social phobia, namely:

* Marked and persistent apprehension about one or more situations in which the individual may be forced to interact with people they do not know or who might judge them. They are afraid of displaying behaviour or symptoms of nerves which may be humiliating or embarrassing for them.
* Strong anxiety, and even a systematic feeling of panic, generated by the simple fact of being in the presence of

other people in certain circumstances.
- The awareness that their fear is excessive and irrational.
- Acute anxiety or profound distress when they avoid or face up to the stressful situation or attention from others that they are afraid of.
- Acute suffering and major disturbances to their day-to-day life as a result of the behaviours adopted to avoid the situations that cause anxiety and of the symptoms experienced.

Specific phobias

Specific phobias involve an irrational, excessive and constant fear of a particular situation or object. The anxiety felt manifests itself as a panic attack and/or avoidant behaviour. In this specific case, it is essential to distinguish clearly between fear and phobias. In the first case, the subject may be afraid of a situation, but will not avoid it; in the second case, the person suffering from the phobia will do everything they can to escape the threat.

The DSM-IV distinguishes between four types of specific phobias:

- **animal type**, which includes, for example, arachnophobia and phobias of snakes or insects;
- **natural environment type**, which includes phobia of heights, water, storms, and so on;
- **blood/injection/injury type**, which comprises phobias such as hematophobia (phobia of blood) and aichmophobia (phobia of needles);
- **situational type**, which includes phobia of planes, lifts,

public places, and so on.

Obsessive-compulsive disorder

Obsessive-compulsive disorder, or OCD, is considered to be an anxiety disorder and involves obsessions and compulsive behaviours. The individual is constantly overwhelmed by unpleasant thoughts which result in feelings of fear, anxiety and even disgust. The sufferer's only way of putting an end to these debilitating feelings is to put in place small, repetitive rituals known as compulsions, which can be very time-consuming.

The most common phobias in this case include phobias of germs and infections, which result in compulsions involving extreme hygiene (showering several times a day, wearing a face mask or gloves, cleaning their room every day) and an obsessive concern for symmetry and organisation which manifests itself as a compulsive need to put every object in a particular place.

Post-traumatic stress disorder (PTSD)

Post-traumatic stress disorder occurs in some people who have experienced or witnessed a traumatic event during which their physical integrity or that of another person may have been threatened. However, it is impossible to genera-lise about the sufferers of PTSD. While some people develop chronic anxiety caused by situations, noises or places that remind them of the traumatic event, others do not expe-rience any symptoms at all. To deal with this overwhelming and debilitating fear, the subject adopts a range of defence mechanisms such as avoidance, denial and hyperactivity, which allow them to avoid reliving these painful moments. However, these solutions are only temporary and do not help with the deep-seated pain at the root of this feeling of powerlessness and panicked fear.

THE ORIGINS OF ANXIETY

As is the case for many illnesses, anxiety does not stem from one single cause, but rather from a combination of factors which, when combined, cause the sufferer to become anxious.

Biological factors

Some people have a genetic predisposition to this kind of illness. Certain genes and hormones seem to encourage the development of anxiety. These include in particular serotonin, a neurotransmitter in the central nervous system, and activin, a hormone which plays a role in the regulation of the menstrual cycle.

As women experience constant hormonal changes, they can prove more sensitive to stress and anxiety, especially at certain points in their hormonal cycle. For example, over the course of the premenstrual period and the menstrual cycle, the levels of three hormones which are essential for general balance (progesterone, testosterone and oestrogen) can fluctuate significantly, even from one day to the next! This can result in anxiety, among other symptoms.

Cortisol, sometimes called the stress hormone, provides

another illustration of the influence of biology on anxiety. When this hormone is mobilised, it takes control of our bodies and can inhibit the activity of our immune system to allow itself to work more effectively.

In other words, our bodies and their many genes and hormones have a multitude of ways of causing anxiety. Nonetheless, although biology does have a real and omnipresent influence on anxiety, it would be much too simplistic to view it as the only cause of the phenomenon without taking into account the individual's environment and development.

Psychosocial factors

Besides the factors which are inherent to the individual, a person's sociocultural environment and experiences will have just as much of an impact on the development of anxiety. Indeed, a natural predisposition will be more likely to develop if the context is favourable. Consequently, a series of events can encourage the emergence of anxiety: a stressful family environment, a dysfunctional parent-child relationship, job loss, divorce, overwork, an accident, a serious illness, and so on.

DEBILITATING SYMPTOMS

While anxiety wears many masks, the symptoms are relatively similar for most anxiety disorders, although they can vary slightly from person to person. This state of constant heightened stress manifests itself on both the psychological and the physical level, doubling victims' suffering.

Psychological and behavioural symptoms

Anxiety disorders reduce the secretion of certain neu-
rotransmitters in the brain. Anxious individuals may also
display elevated levels of activity in the cerebral cortex. As a
result, anxiety leads to many psychological and behavioural
symptoms such as pessimism, hyperactivity, fear of losing
control, emotional detachment, a desire to flee, and so on.

Physical symptoms

Beyond its psychological and behavioural manifestations,
anxiety is characterised by very intense and particularly
debilitating physical symptoms. These include heart palpitations, a feeling of suffocation, nausea, clammy or cold
hands, pins and needles in the limbs, vertigo and tension in
the body.

Of course, not all of these symptoms are present in every
case or last for a long time, and their appearance varies
depending on the kind of anxiety disorder.

> "I was diagnosed as agoraphobic a few years ago. My anxiety
> disorder was not really all that debilitating to begin with:
> it was not there all the time and, when it did appear, I told
> myself it was just because I was tired. However, my anxiety
> attacks gradually became more frequent and intense, and a
> lot of symptoms began to appear: I would get a lump in my
> throat, have violent headaches, begin to hyperventilate, and
> so on, for no apparent reason." (Stephanie, 30)

Health consequences

Anxiety and stress are not pleasant emotions for anyone. However, when anxiety persists or becomes chronic, what was initially just an unpleasant feeling can cause genuine health problems.

In addition, it is difficult to identify the problem because the symptoms of anxiety can resemble the symptoms of other illnesses. For example, if you have a headache you may tell yourself that you must have caught a cold waiting for the bus yesterday, or that the wine you had at dinner was not the best. However, it is possible that the real cause of your pain is anxiety. Anxiety can have a range of consequences for your health, which can vary in visibility and seriousness. When it comes to your mental and physical health, anxiety is anything but harmless!

Physical effects:

- headaches,
- sore throats,
- stomach, digestive and liver problems,
- breathing difficulties,
- skin reactions,
- muscle pain,
- sleep problems,
- bruxism (excessive teeth grinding),
- high blood pressure,
- cardiovascular problems,
- weakened immune system,
- cancer.

Mental and behavioural effects:

- memory problems,
- difficult concentrating,
- mood swings,
- depression,
- alcoholism and drug abuse,
- eating disorders.

HOW CAN YOU AVOID LETTING ANXIETY OVERWHELM YOU?

Treating anxiety may seem simple: it is easy to think that all you have to do is eliminate the source of the problem (work, health, family issues, and so on). However, the solution is actually less straightforward, because running away from the problem is only a temporary remedy, a plaster on an open wound. Having practical tools at your disposal can therefore be particularly useful during a period of crisis.

There are a range of solutions to manage your anxiety. Whether you decide to take steps alone or ask a healthcare professional for help, the important thing is not to let the situation get worse. You should choose the best option for you: a healthy lifestyle, simple relaxation techniques, therapy sessions or medication.

PERSONAL INITIATIVE

A healthy lifestyle

Unsurprisingly, lifestyle plays a vital role in the management of anxiety. You should pay attention to sleep, diet and physical activity in your everyday life.

- **Sleep.** Try to stick to a regular sleep schedule. Going to bed and getting up at the same time as much as possible can considerably improve your mental and physical health. Similarly, make sure that you are getting enough sleep. According to a study by the National Sleep

Foundation, the average adult needs between seven and nine hours' sleep per night to function properly. Pay attention to your needs and respect them.

- **Diet.** Our body is an incredible machine, made up of many different components that need to be fuelled properly. No motor runs correctly without the right fuel. Proteins, fats, vitamins, calcium, magnesium, iron and omega-3 fatty acids are essential to our effective functioning. If you do not eat enough of certain foods, you may cause imbalances in your body and suffer the consequences: lack of energy, lethargy, joint pain... and anxiety. If you feel that you do not know how to adopt a healthy and balanced diet, do not hesitate to consult a nutritionist, who will be able to analyse your food habits and adapt them to your needs. Furthermore, while this might seem obvious, it is important to stress that stimulants (tea, coffee, energy drinks), alcohol and drugs are not a healthy way of managing anxiety. Although your symptoms may seem to lessen at first, these substances only offer a temporary and, above all, an illusionary solution.

> "I had a lot of anxiety attacks and episodes of stress which resulted in insomnia. Then, I got advice about my diet and increased my intake of magnesium, vitamin B, vitamin D and omega-3. It worked miracles! Since I changed my diet, I haven't had any more anxiety attacks or serious stress." (Alice, 35)

- **Physical activity.** Whether as a way of keeping your anxiety under control, staying in shape or simply having fun, regular physical activity is always beneficial for keeping your body and mind healthy. If you are predisposed towards anxiety, exercise will help you to focus your mind on a specific activity and get rid of intrusive thoughts, but also to use up some of your energy and, consequently, your anxiety. When you exercise, your brain releases endorphins, which relieve pain and have similar effects to some opiates. Also known as anti-stress hormones, endorphins result in a feeling of euphoria and mental and physical calm when we take part in physical activity at a comfortable intensity for a long enough period of time. As well as this psychological benefit, exercise also makes your body stronger and healthier. As the Romans said, the key to a balanced life is "a healthy mind in a healthy body" (*Mens sana in corpore sano*).

Good social support

You are undoubtedly already familiar with the anxious state where thoughts constantly swirl around in your head and do not leave you a moment's peace. Before you even think about treating it, it is essential that you learn to recognise it. If you let yourself express your worries, you will be better able to accept their presence and avoid turning them into a shameful secret and burying your head in the sand.

Although some people prefer to deal with their anxiety alone, others need social support. Confiding in a loved one will take a weight off your mind, at least for a moment, and above all will help you feel that you are not alone. Since your friends and family know you well, they are well placed to find the right words to calm you down and help you to put things into perspective, and they will not be afraid to give you their opinions, even if they may be hard for you to hear.

You may be surprised to find out that you are not the only person trapped by anxiety.

Time for yourself

When you feel anxiety rearing its ugly head, switching off from the world and focusing on your needs can help you to keep it under control. This will distract you from your obsessive thoughts and the things that are making you anxious. While some people see this as running away from your problems, temporarily shutting out your worries is a particularly helpful strategy for managing anxiety. There is no point in dwelling on your problems and trying to deal with the thing that is making you stressed if you cannot do so calmly. Your brain will constantly be on high alert and will not let you think clearly about a solution. It is better to do everything in good time: start by setting your mind straight and deal with the problem afterwards.

The best way to do this is to take time for yourself. Give yourself a moment to breathe, get your bearings, take a break in the whirlwind of your everyday life and enjoy some alone time. Even if you feel overwhelmed by tasks and professional and family obligations, give yourself an hour or even just a few minutes, depending on how much time you have available, to do what you want. However, you should avoid using your smartphone, tablet or any other electronic device late at night, because studies have shown that they negatively impact the quality of your sleep.

MEDITATION

More and more people are taking up meditation, which is seen as the ideal practical tool to let go of everyday stress and free yourself from the constant thoughts occupying your mind. While there are now countless different kinds of meditation, we can distinguish between four main types, which each have their own applications, benefits and demands.

or more serious ("Am I happy?", "Why does my boss never praise me? Am I going to be fired?", and so on), this it completely normal! The more you try not to think, the more you will be overwhelmed by reflections and intrusive thoughts. A similar thing happens when we are told to avert our eyes from our television screens so that we do not see a shocking image: we are more drawn to it and tend to do exactly what we were told not to do. Our minds like to contradict us!

Vipassanā meditation

This meditation technique is based on the principle of breathing. With the help of some simple exercises which involve working seriously on breathing, practitioners are able to improve their concentration and attention span. When we are anxious, our breathing becomes short, rapid and irregular. Vipassanā meditation can be particularly useful in helping you to calm down.

ABDOMINAL BREATHING EXERCISE

Sitting either cross-legged or on a chair (the important thing is that you are comfortable), place your hands flat on your stomach and close your eyes. Take a deep breath in, focusing on the passage of air from your nose to your stomach. Every time you breathe in, your stomach should fill with air, before emptying again when you breathe out. Focus your attention on this movement and on the feeling that goes through your body when you are breathing.

Abdominal breathing is ideal for calming stress and anxiety. When we use our ribcage in our breathing, we send a signal of fear to our brain, as this kind of breathing is associated with our survival instinct and therefore with danger. Taking long, deep breaths develops the diaphragm and allows complete, calming breathing.

Transcendental meditation

The technique of transcendental meditation is simple, natural and effortless, and can be carried out in two 20-minute sessions per day. It involves profound relaxation through the use of mantras.

TRANSCENDENTAL MEDITATION EXERCISE

Find a calm place away from external distractions. Sit either cross-legged or on a chair – once again, the important thing is that you are comfortable. Close your eyes, do not try to concentrate and breathe naturally, without thinking. Then, either out loud or in your head, repeat a mantra of your choosing. For example, you could use the following mantra: "I am here and now, and I am good". Without effort, continue to repeat this phrase calmly and slowly. Every time your mind wanders, gently bring it back to your mantra.

Zen meditation or zazen

The word "Zen" means "meditation", and zazen is the seated meditation position practiced in Zen Buddhism. This method helps practitioners to meditate in a seated position in order to reach awakening. The practice is about experiencing the world as it is rather than according to a series of mental expectations and projections. Zen meditation involves experiencing and immediately understanding everything because, thanks to pure observation of what is, we can change our outlook on the world and on reality.

Mindfulness meditation

The aim of this meditation is to focus on the present moment, and therefore to feel and become aware of all your sensations during this moment. As such, every time your attention wanders from its focus point, you need to bring it back to the present moment and your feelings. This practice will allow you to reduce your tendency to judge, better appreciate what the present has to offer you, spend less time dwelling on the past and being afraid of the future and therefore lessen your general anxiety levels.

Make yourself comfortable in a room away from all distractions and lie down. Gently let yourself become aware of your body by focusing on each individual part. Visualise a flow of air passing over your body from your feet to your head. Start with the tips of your toes and slowly move up through your legs, your abdomen, your chest, your arms and your fingertips, before finishing at the top of your head. Start with just a few minutes of meditation, and increase the length of your sessions as your concentration improves.

One advantage of mindfulness is that it can be practiced every day. The aim is to be completely in the present moment and focus on what you are doing here and now in everyday activities. Feel free to use mindfulness when carrying out another activity. When you do a sport, forget about your final goal and the performance and results you want to obtain, but concentrate instead on your breathing, feel each of your movements and stay grounded in the present moment. This exercise is particularly useful in solitary sporting activities such as running, swimming and cycling. If you go hiking in the woods or in a park, focus your attention on the air, the colours, the sounds, and so on. This meditative walking, combined with the spontaneous calm that nature produces, will help you to free yourself from your anxiety and anchor yourself in the present.

Meditation through movement

Alongside these traditional types of meditation, which mainly involve mental exercise, there is a more physical form of meditation which uses both the mind and the body. Its strength lies in the fact that it involves movement: for people who struggle with traditional meditation because it requires physical immobility, relaxation through the body is a good alternative, because the aim is to reach a state of mindfulness through movement. This allows the body to express itself and avoid a kind of stasis which worsens the feeling of loss of control for some anxious people. While these techniques are becoming increasingly popular and diversifying based on demand, we can distinguish between three main practices:

- **Yoga.** The word "yoga" comes from a very old Sanskrit root which means "to join" or "to unite". Yoga aims to unify the external (body and environment) and internal (mind and psyche) sides of the human being. However, you need to be very careful: yoga is a serious and precise discipline that can cause severe injuries if it not practiced correctly. As such, if you are really set on doing yoga alone, you are advised to attend some lessons first so that a qualified yoga instructor can guide you, check your positions and correct them if necessary. This will stop you from developing bad habits.
- **Tai Chi.** Tai Chi is originally from China and is derived from martial arts. It involves a series of continuous, circular movements that are executed precisely and slowly in a set order. Tai Chi practitioners give the impression that they are fighting against thin air, because the move-

ments are a series of gestures from martial arts, which are carried out with the aim of managing energy rather than as part of combat.

- **Qigong.** Although qigong is also from China and involves managing energy, it is not the same as Tai Chi. This practice places greater emphasis on the qi, meaning "life energy", or the energy that is present in all things. Specifically, qigong focuses on breathing and involves slow, gentle movements and stretching exercises, as well as breathing, meditation, visualisation and combat exercises, each of which come from different traditions.

PROFESSIONAL TREATMENT

Consulting a healthcare professional, either because you feel out of your depth on your own or simply because you find talking to another person more helpful, will enable you to carry out in-depth work. Asking for help is never a sign of weakness. Quite the opposite, in fact – by asking for help you are showing your determination to get better and take back control of your life. Besides going to see a therapist, there are now many other alternatives to traditional medicine that can, if not cure you, at the very least help you to minimise certain symptoms.

Therapy

There are three kinds of therapy that can help to treat anxiety: cognitive therapy, behavioural therapy and cognitive behavioural therapy, which combines the two. Cognitive therapy involves exploring our cognitive schema, meaning the mental habits that are stored in our long-term memories as a result of our experiences. Behavioural therapies work on the principle of conditioning, meaning our automatic responses to all stimuli. Finally, cognitive behavioural therapy combines these two principles and gives patients the tools they need to control the symptoms of anxiety, while studying the factors at the root of the feeling.

Treatment through medication

Sometimes, when therapy is not enough, it can be useful to move on to medication. That said, treatment through medication must always be accompanied by in-depth therapeutic treatment which will try to pinpoint the causes of the illness and suggest appropriate long-term solutions, since medication only temporarily relieves the symptoms of anxiety. Using medication alone is therefore not a solution in itself, but can be a temporary help when you urgently need it.

The two most frequently prescribed types of medication for anxiety disorders are anxiolytics and antidepressants. Anxiolytics have the advantage that they act rapidly on symptoms, while antidepressants, particularly selective serotonin reuptake inhibitors (SSRIs) and serotonin-norepinephrine reuptake inhibitors (SNRIs) seem to be preferred by specialists over the medium-term.

Alternative medicine

Sometimes, when an individual's condition is not helped by traditional medicine, some alternative approaches may prove useful. Nowadays, an increasingly large segment of the population is turning to more natural and less invasive treatments for their illnesses. However, although these treatments are well established on the market, you will still need to think critically about them and research recognised practitioners in your area. You could try:

- **Homeopathy.** Although homeopathy is practiced all over the world, it remains highly controversial and is often described as a placebo. It involves treating patients – and not their illness – by administering a small dose of a substance that can cause the same symptoms in a healthy person, following the principle "let like be cured by like".

- **Phytotherapy.** This is a treatment method which uses medicinal plants. There are a range of plants that can help to reduce anxiety. Of course, none of them are a miracle cure, and they are mainly used to lessen mild anxiety. In all cases, these natural remedies will lead to improvements, no matter how intense your anxiety is. Some of the plants you can use include hawthorn, Saint John's wort, camomile, lime, hop, passion flower, valerian, lavender and saffron. Research their effects, uses and possible contraindications before taking any of them.

- **Aromatherapy.** This treatment uses pure essential oils and essences extracted from aromatic plants for their therapeutic properties. Each essential oil has its own specific properties.
- **Sophrology.** This practice, which is sometimes compared to hypnosis, combines relaxation, meditation and self-hypnosis. With the help of mental, breathing and some physical exercises, the patient concentrates intensely on a specific need.
- **Acupuncture.** Acupuncture, which comes from traditional Chinese medicine, involves inserting needles into various precise points on the patient's body in order to relieve certain pains and even to treat illness. Acupuncture is often used as a complement to other treatments, and does not claim to be able to treat serious illnesses.
- **Hypnosis.** This practice involves reproducing a natural and spontaneous hypnotic state. Hypnosis involves intentionally reaching an altered state of consciousness, meaning a state of consciousness where things are perceived differently. Hypnosis can be used to sooth pain and anxiety disorders.
- **Kinesiology.** This physical and mental technique mainly involves using manual muscular tests to identify imbalances in the body. Kinesiology is therefore based on the principle that our minds and bodies are closely linked. Not to be confused with kinesiotherapy!

HOW CAN YOU KEEP YOUR ANXIETY UNDER CONTROL?

Now that you have the tools you need to manage your anxiety better on an everyday basis, how are you going to maintain this balance over the long term? Do not think that you are invincible – some relapses are inevitable. You will sometimes feel out of your depth in a particular situation and will be unable to control your anxiety or the resulting symptoms. However, as long as this only happens occasionally, there is no need to worry.

A FEW FINAL TIPS

Try to apply these few tips in your day-to-day life and, above all, remember how far you have come and the good habits you have already put in place.

- Make sure you stick to a good sleep schedule. Get up and go to bed at a similar time each day.
- Stick to a healthy, balanced diet. If you feel the need, consult a nutritionist, who will help you to establish a full programme.
- Exercise regularly.
- Get some fresh air and sunlight whenever you have the chance.
- Surround yourself with people you trust and do not be afraid to share your worries and fears.
- Take some quiet time for yourself. Give yourself time to breathe.
- When you feel anxiety emerging, take a few slow, deep

breaths, focusing on your breathing and the way it moves through your body.
- Ground yourself in the present moment, and be sensitive to and aware of your surroundings.
- Take up meditation through movement, for example by signing up to a Tai Chi or yoga class.
- Consult a mental health specialist, who will be able to help you lift the weight of anxiety.

FAQS

I AM CONSTANTLY WORRIED AND STRESSED. EVERYTHING MAKES ME ANXIOUS AND THIS SOMETIMES PARALYSES ME. IS THIS NORMAL?

There are different types of anxiety. There is anxiety linked to stress, which is common and completely normal and harmless. This happens to everyone and is nothing to worry about. For example, a problem in your career, a conflict with a friend or family member, or traffic jams making you late will put you more on edge than usual, but you should reassure yourself that this is not a cause for alarm.

Alongside this, there are more serious kinds of anxiety that can prove debilitating. When anxiety becomes chronic and particularly intense, it ends up affecting our balance, our health and our day-to-day behaviour. In this case, you need to face up to the problem and take action to stop your anxiety getting the better of you. Generalised anxiety disorder (GAD) is recognised as an illness by healthcare specialists and involves constant worrying that is out of proportion to the everyday event that triggered it. In this case, it is important to act, because the situation is more serious than common, harmless stress.

IF I AM NATURALLY ANXIOUS, IS THERE REALLY ANYTHING I CAN DO ABOUT IT, SINCE IT IS A PART OF MY TEMPERAMENT?

Of course you can do something! It is true that we are not all born with the same natural aptitudes, and you may be more predisposed than others to be anxious. However, that does not mean that you have to resign yourself to anxiety and do nothing to change your situation!

Think about your strengths and weaknesses and implement measures that will help you to fight the problem, while respecting your natural inclinations. If you would prefer to explore the issue by yourself to start with, that is fine. Deciding to take care of yourself is a good starting point: letting yourself get a good night's sleep, giving yourself a cosy night in to relax with a cup of tea and a good book, preparing some healthy, tasty food, giving yourself a few minutes to meditate, and so on. If you would rather get moving and explore your feelings outside your house, you could sign up for a sports club or a yoga or qigong class. Finally, if you prefer professional support and guidance, feel free to consult a therapist or another wellbeing specialist. There is a world of possibilities to free yourself from your anxiety, so what are you waiting for?

WHEN I HAVE A SUDDEN ANXIETY ATTACK, WHAT CAN I DO TO CALM DOWN?

There are three techniques you can use if you have an anxiety attack:

- **Focus on your breathing.** Take big, deep breaths, as these will gradually help you slow down. Go outside or, if this is not possible, open your windows and take five big, very slow breaths. Focus on the feeling of fresh air, which calms and 'cools down' your body when you breathe it in.
- **Mentally scan your body, one part at a time.** Pay attention to your body and all its parts. Carry out a body scan, from the bottom of your body up to the top. Start with your toes and, very slowly, work your way up step by step to the top of your head, paying attention to and feeling every part of your body.
- **Focus your senses on your surroundings.** Concentrate on each of your senses in turn. What sounds can you hear? What can you smell? How warm is the air on your skin? What are the points of contact between your skin and the things around it (clothes, fabric, chair, ground, and so on)? This will allow you to fix your attention on something and take your mind off your anxiety.

MY PARTNER IS A VERY ANXIOUS PERSON. WHAT CAN I DO TO HELP THEM?

Being overwhelmed by anxiety affects everything in our daily lives, but it can often also affect the people around us. It is generally difficult to limit the negative consequences of our problem for our loved ones. However, an anxious person's loved ones can help them to overcome their anxiety. Whether your partner, your child, another family member or a friend suffers from anxiety, you can help them get better.

- First of all, it is very important to offer support to the anxious person, but it is even more important and far more difficult to offer the right support. Indeed, certain kinds of help may not actually be constructive for the person suffering from anxiety. For example, if you change your behaviour so that your partner never has to confront the sources of their anxiety, this could be counterproductive over the long term. By overprotecting them, you will stop them from making progress and developing. This could even hold them back, because your behaviour will inadvertently reduce their freedom and independence. For example, if the idea of driving makes your partner anxious, getting behind the wheel instead of them every time you are in the car together will not help them in the long term, because you are reinforcing their habit of avoidance. This does not mean that you need to be too strict and never show empathy! Encouraging their avoidant behaviour is not a good idea, but listening and being patient and tolerant are necessary forms of support. Show your anxious partner that you understand and respect them. Communicate gently and listen. Open up a dialogue and emphasise the progress the anxious person has made, rather than their difficulties.

- Next, it is important to avoid focusing solely on their anxiety. Talk to them about other things. Do not make their anxiety a bigger issue than it needs to be by making it your only topic of conversation! Instead, teach your partner to put things into perspective, be open to other areas of life and develop their personality. This will allow them to see themselves as more than just an anxious person.

- Finally, encourage them to ask for help and suggest

accompanying them in this step if they want you to. For example, you could tell them that going with them to a therapy session will give you the opportunity to learn about and get a better understanding of their problem and the things you can do to help them. And if you feel that you need help to support your partner, do not be afraid to consult a specialist or meet people who also have an anxious friend or family member.

We want to hear from you!
Leave a comment on your online library
and share your favourite books on social media!

FURTHER READING

BIBLIOGRAPHY

- American Psychiatric Association. (2013) *Diagnostic and Statistical Manuel of Mental Disorders, Fifth Edition (DSM-5)*. Arlington, Virginia: American Psychiatric Association Publishing.
- André, C. and Muzo. (2010) *Je dépasse mes peurs et mes angoisses*. Paris: Éditions Points.
- Anxiéte.fr. (No date) *Homepage*. [Online]. [Accessed 28 June 2017]. Available from: <https://www.anxiete.fr/>
- Berghmans, C. (2010) *Soigner par la méditation*. Paris: Masson.
- Besançon, G. (1993) *Manuel de psychopathologies – Anxiété, dépression et psychopathologie du corps*. Paris: Dunod.
- Bexton, B. (No date) Le trouble d'anxiété généralisée. *Revivre*. [Online]. [Accessed 28 June 2017]. Available from: <http://www.revivre.org/anxiete/>
- Cabut, S. (2013) Psychiatrie : DSM-5, le manuel qui rend fou. *Le Monde*. [Online]. [Accessed 28 June 2017]. Available from: <http://www.lemonde.fr/sciences/article/2013/05/13/dsm-5-le-manuel-qui-rend-fou_3176452_1650684.html>
- Haute Autorité de Santé. (2007) *La prise en charge de votre trouble anxieux*. [Online]. [Accessed 28 June 2017]. Available from: <https://www.has-sante.fr/portail/upload/docs/application/pdf/2008-06/08-091_tag.pdf>
- National Sleep Foundation. (No date) *How much*

sleep do we really need? [Online]. [Accessed 28 June 2017]. Available from: <https://sleepfoundation.org/how-sleep-works/how-much-sleep-do-we-really-need>
- Servant, D. (2003) *Soigner le stress et l'anxiété par soi-même.* Paris: Éditions Odile Jacob.
- Sommeil et médecine générale. (No date) *Échelle d'Hamilton d'évaluation de l'anxiété.* [Online]. [Accessed 28 June 2017]. Available from: <http://www.sommeil-mg.net/spip/questionnaires/HAM-%20A%20fr.pdf>

ADDITIONAL SOURCES

- Brotheridge, C. (2017) *The Anxiety Solution: A Quieter Mind, A Calmer You.* London: Penguin.
- Lewis, M. (2016) *Overcome Anxiety: A Self Help Toolkit for Anxiety Relief and Panic Attacks.* CreateSpace Independent Publishing Platform.
- Trickett, S. (1996) *Coping with Anxiety and Depression.* London: Sheldon Press.
- Vernon, C. (2016) *Anxiety Rebalance: All the Answers You Need to Overcome Anxiety and Depression.* London: Headline Home.
- Wayne, P. and Fuerst, M. (2013) *The Harvard Medical School Guide to Tai Chi: 12 Weeks to a Healthy Body, Strong Heart, and Sharp Mind.* Boston, Massachusetts: Shambhala Publications Inc.
- Williamson, A. and Newell, R. (2017) *Breaking Mad: The Insider's Guide to Conquering Anxiety.* London: Bloomsburg.

IMPROVE YOUR GENERAL KNOWLEDGE

IN A BLINK OF AN EYE !

www.50minutes.com

Made in the USA
Monee, IL
07 July 2026